My Librarian Is a Camel

How Books Are Brought to Children Around the World

Margriet Ruurs

Boyds Mills Press

For Rob, who loves to travel.
And to all people who bring children and books together.
—M. R.

Text copyright © 2005 by Margriet Ruurs
Photographs: Credits included in acknowledgments on p. 32
All rights reserved.

Published by Boyds Mills Press, Inc.
A Highlights Company
815 Church Street
Honesdale, Pennsylvania 18431
Printed in China
Visit our Web site at www.boydsmillspress.com

Publisher Cataloging-in-Publication Data (U.S)

Ruurs, Margriet.
    My librarian is a camel : how books are brought to children around the world /
by Margriet Ruurs.—1st ed.
[   ] p. : col. ill. ; cm.
ISBN 1-59078-093-0
1. Traveling libraries — Juvenile literature. 2. Librarians — Juvenile literature. I. Title.
027.4 22   Z716.R887 2005

First edition, 2005
The text of this book is set in 12-point Stone Serif.

10 9 8 7 6 5 4 3 2

CONTENTS

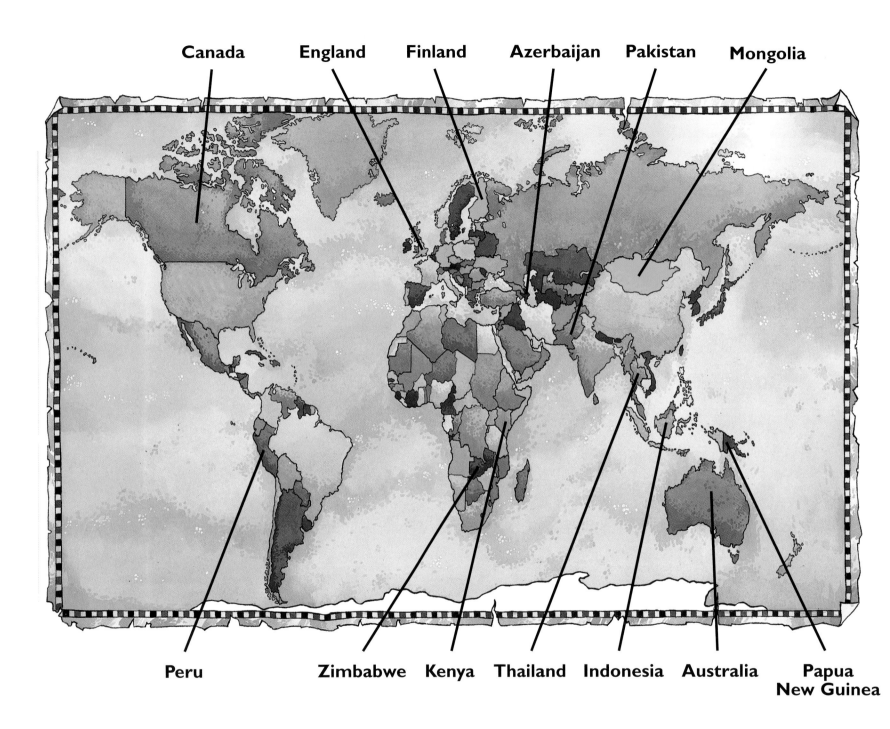

Canada   England   Finland   Azerbaijan   Pakistan   Mongolia

Peru   Zimbabwe   Kenya   Thailand   Indonesia   Australia   Papua New Guinea

INTRODUCTION

Several years ago, I read a newspaper article about a camel in Kenya that was used to bring books to young people who lived in remote desert villages. I wondered how else books might be brought to children in other parts of the world. My research turned up all sorts of "mobile libraries": libraries that moved on legs, on wheels, and by other means.

I was thrilled to learn how far people would go to put books into the hands of young readers. I began to contact librarians in faraway places. They responded by sharing information, personal stories, and photos of their mobile libraries and of the young people who use them. Over time, I assembled a scrapbook of mobile libraries from all over the world.

Developing this book has been a rewarding and exciting experience. From Azerbaijan to Zimbabwe, I discovered people who are passionate about books and who understand the importance of libraries in our lives. One librarian in Azerbaijan explained that the library is "as important as air or water."

Maybe you have been taking your local library for granted, just as I did. Next time you borrow books, think of how lucky you are to be able to choose from all of those free books and to take home as many as you wish.

The librarians and volunteers who bring books by camel or elephant or by boat inspired me. I hope they inspire you, too.

AUSTRALIA

In Australia, there are more than five thousand libraries. About seventy-two of those libraries are on wheels. Some mobile libraries cover the Gold Coast, a strip of beaches in the state of Queensland that runs north from the border with New South Wales toward Brisbane, the state capital. Huge trucks and trailers carry thousands of books to children who cannot go to a library in a city.

Travis, a librarian, travels on one of the trucks. He stops at schools to talk about books and to tell stories.

"Some stories leave children with something to think about," says Travis. "Others bring laughter or tears." Stories can get kids excited about books and reading, so they borrow lots of books.

The mobile library that Travis runs is more than a truck. It is a solar-powered high-tech library. The solar panel is on the top of the truck. Inside are six computers and a printer powered by a UPS (uninterrupted power supply) unit, which is charged from a bank of batteries.

The truck comes with three air-conditioning units, two banks of fluorescent lights, nine spotlights, and a stereo system with surround sound. It also features a wheelchair lift, a microwave oven, a small refrigerator, a toilet, and two sinks. All of these units are powered by a bank of constantly recharging batteries. The solar panel provides a small current to the batteries that keeps them alive and running.

Commonwealth of Australia
Capital: *Canberra*
Estimated population: *20,000,000*

The smallest continent in the world, Australia lies southeast of Asia. Because the continent is in the Southern Hemisphere, the seasons are opposite to those in the Northern Hemisphere. Summer begins on December 1. Winter begins on June 1. The official language is English, but there are also hundreds of Aboriginal languages spoken, the languages of Australia's native people.

Australian readers borrow books from their solar-powered library truck.

AZERBAIJAN

The children in the Kelenterli refugee settlement can't sit still when they know that the blue truck is coming! The blue truck library is here, thanks to the hard work of Relief International, an organization that provides relief to victims of natural disasters and civil conflicts.

These children live in poverty, but the blue library truck brings a surge of happiness and curiosity. "It's a big event when the library comes to town," says the librarian. "It's a bit of happiness for children who normally don't have much to look forward to."

This library-in-a-truck has been bringing books to children for several years. Designed to provide a wide variety of books to young people, two library

When the blue library truck arrives, Azerbaijanian children are eager to get their books.

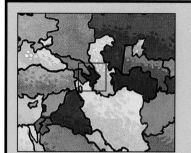

trucks serve over sixteen hundred students in about twenty-three refugee schools. Their goal is simple: for a few hours each week, the children of Kelenterli and other settlements are given the opportunity to borrow books. In doing so, they may feel they are part of a new generation growing up in a new Azerbaijan. The trucks travel through only two regions of Azerbaijan. There are children in other areas of the country who would love to see the blue truck pay them a visit. But unfortunately, there are not enough trucks, or books, to reach them all. Relief International is working to change that.

"For us," says the librarian, "the mobile library is as important as air or water."

Azerbaijani Republic
Capital: *Baku*
Estimated population *8,347,000*

Azerbaijan (Az-ere-bye-SHON) lies in southwest Asia. This former republic of the Soviet Union became independent in 1991. Since the breakup of the Soviet Union, Azerbaijan has been torn by civil conflict. People speak Azerbaijani, but Russian is also spoken, mostly in the capital of the country.

Children in Azerbaijan learn about their country's history through books written in their own language.

9

CANADA

Nunavut, which means "Our Land" in the language of the Inuit people, is a huge territory in Canada's north. The arctic region stretches from the North Pole to Arviat in the south, and from Kugluktuk in the west to Panjnirtung in the east. The distances are huge, and many villages are very isolated. The Northwest Territories reach from Nunavut in the east to the Yukon in the west.

Larger towns like Iqaluit, Tuktoyaktuk, and Yellowknife have their own public-library buildings, but many communities are just too small. Some communities, like Fort Liard, have a virtual library, which offers Internet access. But even if the community does not have any kind of library building, the Northwest Territories public library system offers books to everyone in the far north through their Borrower-by-Mail program.

Tyson Anakvik, Colin Igutaaq, James Naikak, and Cameron Ovilok are friends in Cambridge Bay, Nunavut. They request library books by e-mail or by phone. A mobile library doesn't bring the books to their village; the books are sent through the mail. The Borrower-by-Mail program will send children any books they'd like to read. If the library doesn't have a book in its system, librarians will borrow the book from another library in Canada and mail it. They even include a stamped, addressed envelope, so the children won't have to pay to return the book.

The boys take their young friend Liza for a ride on their sled as they walk to the post office to pick up their books. The boys look forward to reading that night. On winter days, the sun does not come above the horizon, and when the thermometer reads minus 50 degrees, the children like to curl up with a good book by the woodstove. While the northern wind howls across the tundra, they read fantasy and action novels. Liza is excited about finding good picture books in the package.

They can keep their books for up to six weeks. After that, they'll pack them up and walk to the local post office to mail the books back to the library. Then they'll check the mail every day . . . until another big brown package arrives with new books to devour in their remote corner of Canada's Arctic.

Canada
Capital: *Ottawa*
Estimated population: *30,532,900*

Canada, located in North America, is the second-largest country in the world. The most easterly point of Newfoundland is closer to England than it is to Calgary, Alberta. From east to west, Canada is so wide that there are six time zones within its borders. Canada has two official languages, English and French, and native Canadians also speak their own languages. The original people of the North are called Inuit, and they speak Inuktitut.

The Blackpool Library distributes the joy of reading from a wheelbarrow on the beach.

ENGLAND

The Blackpool Beach Library brings books directly to people who are enjoying their summer holiday at the beach. The library is a wheelbarrow!

Two library assistants cart the books up and down the beach. Borrowers needn't join the Blackpool Library. When they finish reading the books, they simply return them to the wheelbarrow when it comes by another day. The people at the Blackpool Library believe that it is important to promote the joy of reading. "Libraries are services, not buildings," says one librarian. So, besides donkey rides and lemonade stands, this beach offers books!

Even a donkey likes to put his nose in a book on the beach.

Gloucester's mobile library.

England
Capital: *London*
Estimated population: *47,000,000*

England is part of the United Kingdom of Great Britain and Northern Ireland. The United Kingdom lies off the northwestern coast of Europe. England, Wales, Scotland, and Northern Ireland form the United Kingdom. The official language is English, but some people in Wales speak Welsh, and some people in Scotland speak Gaelic.

England has other types of mobile libraries as well. Share-a-Book is a children's mobile library van in Gloucester, a county in England. A librarian travels with the van to the countryside, where children don't have access to a regular public library. Many children don't have books at home to read and share with their parents.

Share-a-Book has special books for children for whom English is a second language. They also offer toddler story times and take part in special celebrations in the area.

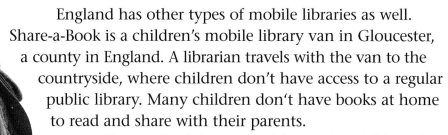

Inside the Share-a-Book library, kids and grown-ups love to share books.

FINLAND

The south coast of Finland skirts the Gulf of Finland. The archipelago, in the southwest, consists of thousands of rocky islands. Some islands have only summer visitors, but others are populated year-round. People in this area of Finland speak both Finnish and Swedish. Since 1976, the

In the middle of Aboland Archipelago is a big water called Gullkrona, meaning "Golden Crown." It was given its name by Queen Blanka of Namur (1316–1363). According to an old legend, while on a voyage to Finland, Queen Blanka promised her golden crown to the most beautiful thing she would see along the way. This turned out to be the bay in the south of Finland, and so she let her crown sink into the waves! The bay is now called Gullkrona Bay.

Pargas Library has been bringing books to the people of these islands by book boat: *Bokbåt* in Swedish or *Kirjastovene* in Finnish.

The boat, called *Kalkholm*, meaning "Limestone Island" in Swedish, measures 4 meters wide and 12 meters long. It carries about six hundred books. The boat, with a crew consisting of a librarian and an assistant, sails among the islands, making about ten stops. Kids come scrambling down the rocky shores to collect their books. Since winters are severe in Finland, the boat goes out only from May to October.

Maj-Len, the chief librarian in Pargas Stad, oversees the operation of the book boat. "Reading has become very important to our book-boat children," she says. "If the book boat didn't come, they might not be reading at all. They are always happy to see us and their supply of new books."

Republic of Finland
Capital: *Helsinki*
Estimated population: *5,156,000*

Finland lies in North Europe. At least a third of the country is north of the Arctic Circle. It is known as "the land of lakes and islands" for good reason. Finland has more than fifty-five thousand lakes, and many thousands of islands. The country has two official languages, Finnish and Swedish. Other languages include Lappish and Romany.

Lapland is a region that stretches across Norway, Sweden, Finland, and part of Russia. Most of Lapland is within the Arctic Circle, and parts of it are under snow and ice year-round. Nomadic Lapps have lived here since the first millennium B.C. Most Lapps are now settled, but some still lead nomadic lives and still depend on reindeer for food, clothes, and shelter.

In Northern Lapland, four towns share a mobile library bus, which also carries children's books. What makes this bus special is that the service is shared by communities in three countries: Finland, Sweden, and Norway.

INDONESIA

Children from villages along the river come running when Indonesia's floating library tugs into sight.

Among the many islands of Indonesia, rivers are the main means of transportation. So it is no wonder that some libraries here float on rivers.

The country has seven floating libraries. The Kalimantan Floating Library consists of a wooden boat, 8 meters long and 3 meters wide. The boat, which is powered by a diesel engine, can carry up to five hundred books.

When the boat first began bringing books to the villages along the river Kahayun, it had to stay until people finished reading their books. That took too much time, so the librarians decided to leave behind containers filled with books. This allowed them to continue traveling the river, bringing books to other villages. Now the children in the villages along the river come running when the library boat tugs upstream. They are all excited about rummaging through a new box of books to read.

In the city of Surabaya, a bicycle library makes its rounds every day. The East Java Library Board decided that a bicycle was the most economical way to deliver books to readers. The library is powered by man and environmentally friendly. The bicycle makes it easy to get around the narrow, winding streets of the city. It carries books and promotes reading around the city, at schools in the countryside, in villages and kampongs, which are urban communities designed to look like villages in the countryside. Children and their parents can borrow books from the bicycle library and exchange them the next time the library visits.

Republic of Indonesia
Capital: *Jakarta*
Estimated population: *238,000,000*

Indonesia consists of many islands. It is the largest group of islands in the world, consisting of more than 17,500 islands that lie between the Indian and Pacific Oceans. The islands of Indonesia include Sumatra, Borneo, Java, Bali, Timor, and many more. The people speak a language called Bahasa Indonesian, but there are also more than two hundred other languages spoken, including English.

In Surabaya, children and adults gather around a bicycle library.

These young readers are grateful for the books brought by camel.

KENYA

The roads to Bulla Iftin, two hundred miles northeast of Nairobi, are impassable because of the desert sand, even for cars with four-wheel drive. But young people who live in nomadic villages in the area are hungry for books. So librarians use the most economical means of transportation — camels!

Library camels are on the road five days a week. They can carry heavy loads and need little water in the heat of the desert. One camel may carry as many as five hundred books, weighing about four hundred pounds. A driver and a librarian divide the books into two boxes. They saddle them on the camel's back, which is covered with a grass mat for protection. A second camel carries a tent that serves as the library roof.

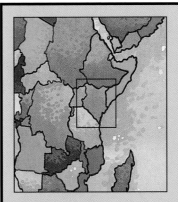

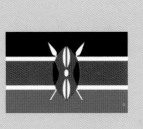

Republic of Kenya
Capital: *Nairobi*
Estimated population: *32,000,000*

Kenya is a country in East Africa. Kenya's climate varies. The coast, which lies on the Indian Ocean, is hot and humid. Inland, the climate is temperate, but the northern part of the country is dry. The official language is English. The national language is Kiswahili.

The students of Bulla Iftin eagerly await the arrival of the camels. When the library caravan finally reaches the village, the children watch as the librarian pitches the tent and displays the books on wooden shelves. The librarian places the grass mats on the ground in the shade of an acacia tree, making a place where the children can sit. The students can treasure their new books for two weeks. When the library camels return, the children can trade their books for new ones.

These camels are ready to bring books to children in remote villages.

19

MONGOLIA

For centuries, people in Mongolia have led a nomadic lifestyle, moving across the steppe, a vast grass-covered plain, with their herds. Many people are still herders of livestock, moving with their herds as they graze. The life of the nomads has not changed very much since the old days except that nowadays the herders like to use "iron horses," meaning motorbikes, instead of real horses. Very few people have telephones, television, or access to computers, but most people can read! There is almost no illiteracy in this country.

Jambyn Dashdondog is a well-known writer of children's books in Mongolia. He was looking for a way to bring books to the many children of herders' families, who live scattered across the Gobi Desert. A horse-drawn wagon (as well as a camel) is used to carry books into the desert.

Mongolian readers reading a book right in their library!

Together with the Mongolian Children's Cultural Foundation, Mr. Dashdondog was able to obtain a minibus and ten thousand books, mostly donated by Japan. The Japanese books are being translated into Mongolian, and Mr. Dashdondog makes trips with the minibus to bring the books to children in the countryside.

The book tour is called *Amttai Nom* which means "candy books." Why? Because before they share the books, the children are given food, including some sweets. After the children listen to stories and choose books, Mr. Dashdondog asks: "Which was sweeter: books or candies?" And the children always answer: "BOOKS!"

"I just returned from a trip to visit herders' children in the Great Gobi Desert," said Mr. Dashdondog, who has visited nearly ten thousand children in the past two years. "We covered some fifteen hundred kilometers in two weeks. And this was in winter, so it was cold and snowy. We had no winter fuel for our bus, so we had to use summer fuel, and the fuel froze at night, making the bus stall. But we weren't cold: the stories and their heroes kept us warm!"

Mongolia
Capital: *Ulaanbaatar*
Estimated population: *2,300,000*

Mongolia is a vast country in northeast Asia, more than one and a half million square kilometers in size. With fewer than two and a half million people living in it, there is lots of empty space throughout the land. The official language is Khalkha Mongol.

To preserve traditional culture and traditions, children are being taught the old Cyrillic Mongolian script, which is written vertically from top to bottom.

The country has high mountain ranges as well as vast desert plains, with the Gobi Desert in the southeast. Snow leopards, wild horses, and ibex still roam the Gobi Desert. Most of the roads that run through Mongolia are unpaved and rough. The climate is one of extremes: cold in winter, hot and very dry in summer.

Even five thousand years ago, nomadic people lived in the area we now call Mongolia.

The country has been in existence since the thirteenth century, when Ghengis Khan conquered a huge part of Europe and Asia. The boundaries have often changed under the rule of China and Russia. Since 1924, the Mongolian People's Republic has been an independent country with its own constitution.

PAKISTAN

There are not many libraries in Pakistan, and libraries for children are especially rare. Most schools don't have libraries either. That is why the Alif Laila Bookbus Society ran a children's library in an old double-decker bus. But in order to reach more children, they needed to put a mobile library on the road. Thanks to help from the Jersey and Guernsey Trust and the United Kingdom's Save the Children, they now have a very popular bus that travels to schools. The bus is called *Dastangou*, or Storyteller.

The bus carries about six thousand books in English and Urdu (the two official languages of Pakistan) to children in schools. Some schools get a weekly visit, but in most places, the Storyteller can come only once every two weeks. This bus full of books has opened up a whole new world to children.

Before the storyteller bookbus came, these Pakistani children didn't have access to books.

THE STORY TELLER......

ALIF LAILA CHILDREN'S LIBRARY

22

Afshan, thirteen, says, "I didn't know what a library looked like before! This bus is magic! It brings stories and books. I just wish it came more often or stayed longer!"

Bushna, from eighth grade, says, "When the Storyteller arrives at the gates of our school, we file out of the school in orderly lines and find our books. Then we take them back to our classrooms to read for an hour."

Mrs. Syeda Basarat Kazim is the coordinator of Storyteller. She explains that there aren't enough books to allow the children to take books home. "If we did, there wouldn't be enough books to take to the next school."

Tabbassum, twelve, says, "The first time the Storyteller came, I ran to it and picked up a book of poetry. I started copying verses from it because I didn't know if it would ever come again. But then Miss Nosheen, who travels with the bus, told me not to worry. It would visit every Tuesday. That really made me happy!"

All that Dastangou *needs now is more books on the shelves.*

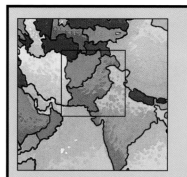

Pakistan
Capital: *Islamabad*
Estimated population: *150,000,000*

Pakistan, an Islamic republic in southern Asia, is bordered by the Arabian Sea, India, Iran, Afghanistan, and China.

The country is twice the size of California and its climate ranges from hot and dry desert in the south to arctic regions in the north. Ethnic groups in Pakistan include Punjabi, Sindhi, Pashtun, and Baloch. Religions included Muslim, Christian, and Hindu.

The official language spoken in Pakistan is called Urdu, and English is the second official language. Other languages spoken include Punjabi, Sindhi, Siraiki, Pashtu, Balochi, Hindko, Brahui, and Burushaski.

Alif Laila, which sponsors the book bus, is an organization dedicated to children's education. The name fits well with a library. Alif Laila wa-Laila is the Arabic title of The Thousand and One Nights. *In this classic collection of tales, the king has sentenced Scherazade to death in the morning. The night before her execution she tells the king a story. The story is so exciting that he wants to hear another. Thus, by telling stories night after night, Scherazade saves her life.*

PAPUA NEW GUINEA

In Papua New Guinea, no roads lead to the remote jungle hamlets or to the schools that serve them. Volunteers from Hope Worldwide, a non-profit charitable organization based in Philadelphia, are committed to bringing books to people in this area of Papua New Guinea. They begin their journey in a four-by-four truck, on a road cut into the steep hillside. After a long, bumpy ride, they eventually come to a village called Mogi-agi, which means "up-and-down road," a perfect description for the surrounding landscape.

At Mogi-agi, students and their teacher file out of the school to greet the volunteers. They are all excited about receiving a new supply of books. But the volunteers aren't done yet. They still have to reach a further destination deeper in the jungle: the village of Amia. They ford a river in their truck and drive until they can go no farther. Then they unload the boxes of books to take them to the small villages in the highlands. From here they must walk for four hours, up the pass and over several ridges, crossing log bridges while carrying the boxes of books on their shoulders. They head up the valley to where the trail stops. Along the way, people who live along the trail bring sugarcane to the volunteers.

The smile of a child holding a book is enough reward for the volunteers who carry boxes of books into the jungle of Papua New Guinea.

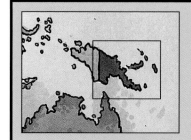

Independent State of Papua New Guinea
Capital: *Port Moresby*
Estimated population: *5,000,000*

Papua New Guinea (Pah-Poo-Ah New Gee-Nee) lies in the Pacific Ocean. It consists of around eight hundred islands just north of Australia and east of Indonesia. The terrain is rugged, with deep valleys and gorges. Most of the country is covered by tropical rain forest. Although the official language is English, over seven hundred other languages are spoken.

When they finally reach Amia, young people come running to meet them. The volunteers have come to help them start a library. The young people help carry books and supplies into the school. The volunteers have brought over a hundred books on their backs. And books are not the only things they deliver. They also bring desperately needed medicines, such as antibiotics and aspirin. The people of Amia gratefully read their books and look forward to the next supply!

So many happy readers in Papua New Guinea.

25

PERU

Children in Peru can receive their books in several different, innovative ways.

CEDILI – IBBY Peru is an institution that delivers books in bags to families in Lima. Each bag contains twenty books, which families can keep for a month. The books come in four different reading levels so that children really learn how to read. The project in Spanish is called *El Libro Compartido en Familia* and enables parents to share the joy of books with their children.

26

In small, rural communities, books are delivered in wooden suitcases and plastic bags. These suitcases and bags contain books that the community can keep and share for the next three months. The number of books in each suitcase depends on the size of the community. There are no library buildings in these small towns, and people gather outside, in the plaza, to see the books they can check out. In the coastal regions, books are sometimes delivered by donkey cart. The books are stored in the reading promoter's home.

In the ancient city of Cajamarca, reading promoters from various rural areas select and receive a large collection of books for their area. The program is called *Aspaderuc*. The reading promoter lends these books to his or her neighbors, and after three months, a new selection of books goes out to each area. Books in this system are for children and adults.

And last but not least, *Fe Y Alegria* brings a collection of children's books to rural schools. The books are brought from school to school by wagon. The children, who are excited about browsing through the books when they arrive, are turning into avid readers.

Some Peruvian readers receive their books by donkey cart.

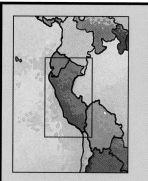

Republic of Peru
Capital: *Lima*
Estimated population: *28,000,000*

Peru, in South Amercia, borders the South Pacific Ocean, between Ecuador and Chile. The tropical coast, the Andes Mountains, and the Amazon River make Peru a diverse and interesting country. The Peruvian people speak Spanish. Quechua is the country's other official language. Peru's history includes the Inca civilization, which occupied much of the South American continent five hundred years ago.

THAILAND

In Omkoi, a region of northern Thailand, there are no schools or libraries. Tribal people cannot read or write. The government of Thailand hopes to change that with a literacy program that includes bringing books to remote villages in the jungle.

A number of these villages can be reached only on foot. This makes transportation difficult, especially during the rainy season. How do you get books to people who need them most, when they live in hard-to-reach mountainous regions of northern Thailand? Elephants!

The elephant library is headed for remote villages in northern Thailand.

The Chiangmai Non-Formal Education Center had the idea to use elephants as libraries. Elephants are already being used here to plow the paddy fields and to carry logs and crops. Now more than twenty elephants in the Omkoi region are used to carry books. The elephant teams spend two to three days in each village. Each trip covers seven or eight villages, so it takes each elephant team eighteen to twenty days to complete a round-trip.

The Books-by-Elephant delivery program serves thirty-seven villages, providing education for almost two thousand people in the Omkoi region. They have even designed special metal slates that won't break when carried on the elephants' backs across the rough terrain.

These slates are used to teach Thai children to write and read. (There are also two-person teams carrying books to about sixteen villages, bringing learning materials to another six hundred people.)

In Bangkok, the capital of Thailand, old train carriages have been transformed into a library. The train is called *Hong Rotfai Yoawachon*, which means "Library Train for Young People." The train serves the homeless children of Bangkok. The Railway Police Division in Bangkok realized there was a need for a safe place for street children, so they refurbished the old train carriages at the railway station, where many of the kids were hanging out. The police restored the trains to their old glory, complete with wood paneling and shining copper light fixtures. They turned the railway cars into a library and a classroom. Here the children learn to read and write. The police have even transformed the area around the train into a garden, where they grow herbs and vegetables.

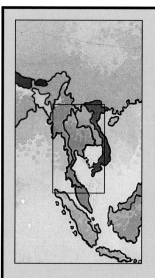

Kingdom of Thailand
Capital: *Bangkok*
Estimated population:
62,860,000

Thailand (Tie-land), which means "the land of the free," lies in Southeast Asia. The climate varies from season to season: dry in January and February, hot in March and May, wet from June to October, and cool in November and December. The official language of the country is Thai.

ZIMBABWE

Many small communities are spread throughout rural Zimbabwe. Bulawayo is a city within the Bulawayo province in western Zimbabwe between North and South Matabeleland provinces. Outside of Bulawayo, there are few paved roads. People travel either on foot or by donkey cart along the sandy trails. And donkey carts carry library books as well.

Rachel, a library volunteer, worked in Bulawayo. Once a week she would load boxes of books onto a small wooden cart drawn by a donkey: the Nkayi Donkey Mobile Library Cart. The Rural Libraries and Resources Development Programme is hoping to nurture reading skills among the young people of rural Zimbabwe. The donkey cart can reach small communities that are inaccessible to vehicles because of the bad roads. Boxes of books delivered by donkey cart are left at schools in different communities for a month at a time.

"We would load boxes of books into the cart," Rachel says, "and walk for hours along the dusty roads to reach different villages. We'd leave the books in the local schools. Then the children and adults would come to the schools to check out the books. We tried to keep the library running on a regular schedule." Rachel adds, laughing, "But sometimes we couldn't catch the donkeys, and then we'd be late!"

One of the Rural Libraries and Resources Programme's brand-new carts is a donkey-driven electro-communications library cart! It brings not only books but also a solar-powered

Librarians promote literacy in rural Zimbabwe.

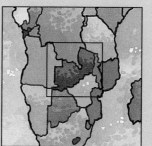
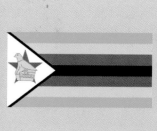

Republic of Zimbabwe
Capital: *Harare (Salisbury)*
Estimated population: *12,833,000*

Zimbabwe (zim-BAHB-way), a landlocked country in southern Africa, is bordered by Botswana, Mozambique, South Africa, and Zambia. Most of Zimbabwe consists of high plateau, known as the High Veld. The official language is English, but people also speak Shona and Ndebele, native languages from the Bantu family of languages.

TV and VCR to children who have never watched TV in their lives. The library plans to add a computer and satellite dish to bring Internet and fax capabilities to this semiarid region of Zimbabwe in the near future.

Rachel was not surprised that the children enjoyed picture books. Since this is an agricultural society, older readers want books on farming. Books in the native Ndebele language are very popular, as are good books from the West. But the children like African literature the best, even if it is in English.

Children in Zimbabwe, like children everywhere, love a good book to read.

ACKNOWLEDGMENTS

The author wishes to thank the following individuals, institutions, and organizations for their generous assistance in the development of this book:

Australia: Travis LeCouteur; John Foster
Azerbaijan: Tarlan Gorchu, Chief Coordinator, TUTU Children's Cultural Center; Farah Adjalova, Permanent Mission of Azerbaijan to the United Nations
Canada: Carol Rigby, Nunavut; Kim Crockatt, Nunavut; Kevin Lafferty, Northwest Territories Public Library System; Christine Drennen, Bowling Green University
England: Elaine Midgley, Blackpool Library; Wheelbarrow project photos courtesy of *The Gazette*, Blackpool; Andrew Fripp, Librarian, Share-a-Book, Gloucestershire; Ian Stringer, Support Services Officer, Central Library; Jake Selwood, Duke University
Finland: Maj-Len Backlund, Chief Librarian, Pargas; Maija Korhonen, Children's Librarian, Helsinki City Library; photo by Camilla Andersén.
Indonesia: R. Natadjumena and Joko Santoso; photos courtesy of The National Library of Indonesia; Murti Bunanta
Kenya: Thelma H. Tate; photos courtesy of IFLA, Kenya National Library Service and the Thomas Moroney Bookmobile Company; Job K. Cherutich, Embassy of Kenya
Mongolia: Jambyn Dashdondog and the Metropolitan Central Library of Ulaanbaatar; Mongolian Mission to the United Nations
Pakistan: Syeda Basarat Kazim; Embassy of Pakistan
Papua New Guinea: Dr. Graham Ogle, Regional Director (South Pacific), HOPE Worldwide; Embassy of Papua New Guinea
Peru: Lilly C. de Cueto, President, IBBY-Peru; Teresa Falcon, CEDILI-IBBY Peru
Thailand: Aree Cheunwattana, Srinakharinwirot University, Bangkok, and Surapong Chaiwong, Chaiwong Non-formal Education Center; Montatip Krishnama, The University of Michigan
Zimbabwe: Maggie Hite; Kenlee Ray; Rachel Elley; Thelma Tate and Professor Lawton; Mr. Matambo, Consulate of Zimbabwe; and Sjoerd Koopman, Coordinator of Professional Activities, International Federation of Library Associations and Institutions

References:
Children's Book News, Canadian Children's Book Centre, Spring 2001
Bookbird, International Board on Books for Young People, Vol. 39, No. 1, 2001; Vol. 39, No. 2, 2001; Vol. 35, No. 2, 1997
"Report on the Assessment of Non-Motorized Mobile Libraries: The Donkey Drawn Mobile Library Services in Zimbabwe," August 6-13, 2001. This Field Study No. 2 was directed by Thelma H. Tate, Chairperson of the Round Table on Mobile Libraries in association with Secretary General Obadiah T. Moyo of the Rural Libraries and Resources Development Programme: a team of professional library experts from institutions in Zimbabwe; and the Thomas Moroney Bookmobile Company (USA).